DEADLY DISASTERS

THE HAITI EARTHQUAKE

BY NATHAN SOMMER

BELLWETHER MEDIA • MINNEAPOLIS, MN

Torque brims with excitement
perfect for thrill-seekers of all kinds.
Discover daring survival skills, explore
uncharted worlds, and marvel at mighty
engines and extreme sports. In *Torque* books,
anything can happen. Are you ready?

This edition first published in 2022 by Bellwether Media, Inc.

Library of Congress Cataloging-in-Publication Data

Names: Sommer, Nathan, author.
Title: The Haiti earthquake / by Nathan Sommer.
Description: Minneapolis, MN : Bellwether Media, 2022. | Series: Deadly
    disasters | Includes bibliographical references and index. | Audience:
    Ages 7-12 | Audience: Grades 4-6 | Summary: "Amazing photography
    accompanies engaging information about the Haiti earthquake. The
    combination of high-interest subject matter and light text is intended
    for students in grades 3 through 7"– Provided by publisher.
Identifiers: LCCN 2021020930 (print) | LCCN 2021020931 (ebook) | ISBN
    9781644875285 (library binding) | ISBN 9781648344367 (ebook)
Subjects: LCSH: Haiti Earthquake, Haiti, 2010–Juvenile literature.
Classification: LCC HV600 2010 .H2 S66 2022 (print) | LCC HV600 2010 .H2
    (ebook) | DDC 363.34/95097294–dc23
LC record available at https://lccn.loc.gov/2021020930
LC ebook record available at https://lccn.loc.gov/2021020931

Editor: Kieran Downs   Designer: Josh Brink

Printed in the United States of America, North Mankato, MN.

TABLE OF CONTENTS

PAUL'S RESCUE

The floor suddenly shook in four-year-old Paul Derlens's apartment. The walls crumbled around him. Paul became trapped beneath them. He cried for help for three days.

Rescuers finally heard Paul's voice on the third day. They spent hours using their hands to dig him out. Paul is one of the survivors of the Haiti earthquake!

RESCUERS

FIRST RUMBLES

FAULT

Tectonic plates make up Earth's **crust**. The plates move very slowly. They meet along **faults**. Sometimes they get stuck. Earthquakes happen when the stuck plates slip. The ground can shake and split open.

Many earthquakes last less than 1 minute. The longest are felt for 10 minutes!

HOW AN EARTHQUAKE BEGINS

CRUST

FAULT

TECTONIC PLATES

HARD TO SEE COMING

Scientists study faults. They know where earthquakes are most likely to happen. But they do not know when they will happen!

The Haiti earthquake began on January 12, 2010. The **epicenter** was around 15 miles (24 kilometers) from the city of Port-au-Prince. More than 2.6 million people lived in and around the city. The main earthquake shook the ground for around 30 seconds. Its **aftershocks** were felt as far away as Cuba and Venezuela!

PORT-AU-PRINCE

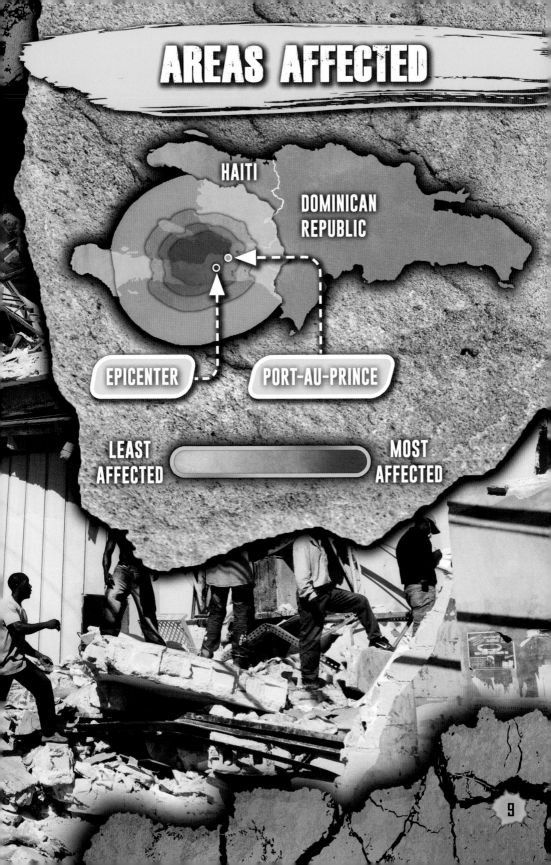

AREAS AFFECTED

HAITI

DOMINICAN REPUBLIC

EPICENTER

PORT-AU-PRINCE

LEAST AFFECTED

MOST AFFECTED

9

The earthquake's **magnitude** was 7.0. Buildings were not strong enough to stand against an earthquake this powerful. Thousands crumbled in seconds.

Haiti's government did not have a plan for large earthquakes. Many Haitians were not trained on earthquake safety. They did not know what to do as the ground shook.

EARTHQUAKE MAGNITUDE SCALE

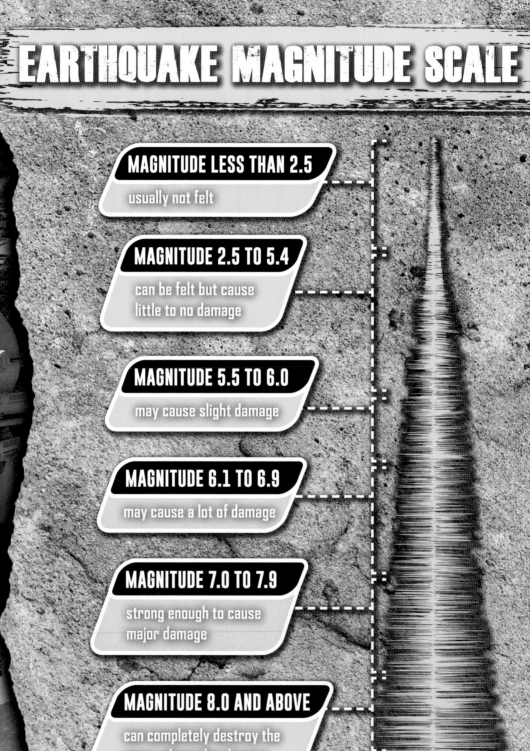

MAGNITUDE LESS THAN 2.5

usually not felt

MAGNITUDE 2.5 TO 5.4

can be felt but cause little to no damage

MAGNITUDE 5.5 TO 6.0

may cause slight damage

MAGNITUDE 6.1 TO 6.9

may cause a lot of damage

MAGNITUDE 7.0 TO 7.9

strong enough to cause major damage

MAGNITUDE 8.0 AND ABOVE

can completely destroy the areas where they happen

DAMAGE AND DESTRUCTION

The Haiti earthquake destroyed more than 106,000 homes. Thousands of lives were lost. Many Haitians were trapped beneath the **rubble**. Every hospital in Port-au-Prince was damaged. This made treating wounded people very hard.

Most of the city's roads and airports were also ruined. Helpers could not easily reach the people in need.

CLOSE TO THE SURFACE
Earthquakes can begin around 500 miles (804 kilometers) underground. Haiti's earthquake began only 6.2 miles (10 kilometers) underground.

The earthquake knocked out electricity in most of Port-au-Prince. Many Haitians could not call for help or reach lost family members. It took many weeks to get the help they needed.

Aftershocks caused further damage. Eight struck on the day of the earthquake. Many more followed in the weeks after the disaster.

A LOT OF EARTHQUAKES

There are around 500,000 earthquakes each year. Around 100,000 can be felt. Only about 100 cause damage!

The earthquake left more than one million people homeless. Large camps for them quickly popped up around Port-au-Prince. Many of these still remain today.

Around 4,000 schools in the area were ruined. Many businesses were also destroyed. Families struggled to return to normal life. The disaster caused $8.5 billion in damage.

ARTIBONITE RIVER

THE ARTIBONITE RIVER

After the earthquake, people had trouble finding clean water. The Artibonite River was dirty. Around 770,000 people became sick after drinking from it.

THE WORLD HELPS HAITI

Countries worldwide sent doctors and supplies to Haiti. **Shelter** and clean water were most needed. Many people gave money. **Relief groups** raised $43 million in text message **donations**.

Survivors used **social media** to find missing family members. It took more than three years to clean up Port-au-Prince. Many buildings were rebuilt after seven years.

TIMELINE

JANUARY 12, 2010

A magnitude 7.0 earthquake strikes 15 miles (24 kilometers) from Port-au-Prince and lasts around 30 seconds

JANUARY 13, 2010

The Dominican Republic is the first country to arrive to help

JANUARY 20, 2010

A magnitude 5.9 aftershock earthquake strikes, causing many damaged buildings to fall

RELIEF GROUP HELPING WITH CLEANUP

OCTOBER 2010

Dirty water from the Artibonite River sickens many survivors

MAY 2013

Most of the rubble from the earthquake has been cleaned up

LONG-TERM EFFECTS

Haiti improved its hospitals after the earthquake. But the country still feels the effects of the disaster. Many homes still need to be rebuilt.

Haiti's government now watches faults more closely. People learn earthquake survival skills. With more knowledge, they are better prepared for future earthquakes!

PREPARATION KIT

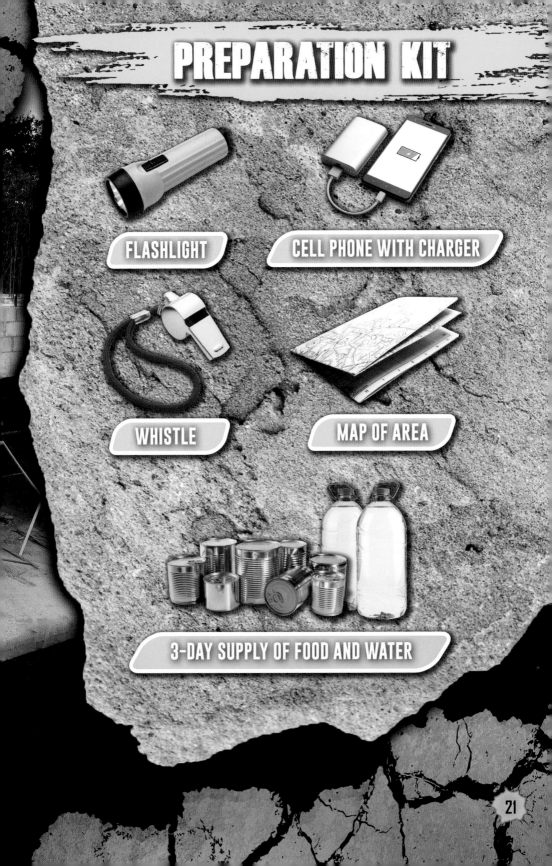

FLASHLIGHT

CELL PHONE WITH CHARGER

WHISTLE

MAP OF AREA

3-DAY SUPPLY OF FOOD AND WATER

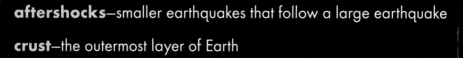

GLOSSARY

aftershocks—smaller earthquakes that follow a large earthquake

crust—the outermost layer of Earth

donations—gifts of money people give to help others in need

epicenter—the part of Earth's surface right above where an earthquake begins

faults—the breaks in Earth's crust that separate tectonic plates

magnitude—the power of an earthquake

relief groups—groups that work to help people affected by disasters

rubble—pieces of rocks, buildings, and garbage that remain after something is destroyed

shelter—a place that offers protection from bad weather or danger

social media—websites people use to stay in contact with each other

tectonic plates—the layers of Earth's crust that move

TO LEARN MORE

AT THE LIBRARY

Light, Charlie. *Earthquakes Reshape Earth.* New York, N.Y.:
Gareth Stevens Publishing, 2021.

London, Martha. *Looking Inside Earth.* Mankato, Minn.:
The Child's World, 2020.

McGregor, Harriet. *Flattened by an Earthquake!* Minneapolis,
Minn.: Bearport Publishing, 2021.

ON THE WEB

FACTSURFER

Factsurfer.com gives you
a safe, fun way to find
more information.

1. Go to www.factsurfer.com

2. Enter "Haiti earthquake" into the search box
   and click 🔍.

3. Select your book cover to see a list of related content.

INDEX